LET'S
see

Mount Rushmore

by Dana Meachen Rau

Content Adviser: Professor Sherry L. Field, Department of Social Science Education,

College of Education, The University of Georgia

Reading Adviser: Dr. Linda D. Labbo, Department of Reading Education,

College of Education, The University of Georgia

Compass Point Books

Minneapolis, Minnesota

Compass Point Books
3722 West 50th Street, #115
Minneapolis, MN 55410

Visit Compass Point Books on the Internet at *www.compasspointbooks.com* or e-mail your
request to *custserv@compasspointbooks.com*

Photographs ©: Lynn Gerig/Tom Stack and Associates, cover; Stock Montage, 4; Charlie Palek/Tom Stack and
Associates, 6; Henryk T. Kaiser/Photo Network, 8; Underwood and Underwood/Corbis, 10, 14; Archive Photos, 12,
16; Unicorn Stock Photos/Phyllis Kedl, 18; James P. Rowan, 20.

Editors: E. Russell Primm and Emily J. Dolbear
Photo Researcher: Svetlana Zhurkina
Photo Selector: Phyllis Rosenberg
Designer: Melissa Voda

Library of Congress Cataloging-in-Publication Data
Rau, Dana Meachen, 1971–
  Mount Rushmore / by Dana Meachen Rau.
    p. cm. — (Let's see library. Our nation)
  Includes bibliographical references and index.
  ISBN 0-7565-0141-5 (lib. bdg.)
  1. Mount Rushmore National Memorial (S.D.)—Juvenile literature. [1. Mount Rushmore National Memorial
  (S.D.) 2. National monuments.] I. Title. II. Series.
  F657.R8 R38 2001
  978.3'93—dc21   2001001590

Table of Contents

Who Made Mount Rushmore?

Some people in South Dakota wanted to make a **monument** that would bring visitors to their state. In 1925, they asked Gutzon Borglum to make it for them.

Borglum was born in Idaho Territory in 1867. He studied art in Paris. He liked to carve large sculptures. Making a monument in South Dakota seemed like a great idea to Borglum.

◄ *Gutzon Borglum dreamed of a great sculpture in South Dakota.*

Where Is Mount Rushmore?

Borglum hiked through the Black Hills in South Dakota looking for a good spot to carve the monument. He found a large mountain made of granite called Mount Rushmore. He decided that Mount Rushmore was big enough, flat enough, and strong enough for the monument.

Mount Rushmore is 25 miles (40 kilometers) southwest of Rapid City, South Dakota.

◄ *Borglum found the perfect place for his sculpture in the Black Hills.*

Who Is Carved on Mount Rushmore?

Borglum decided to carve the faces of four U.S. presidents on the mountain. He chose George Washington, Thomas Jefferson, Abraham Lincoln, and Theodore Roosevelt.

Washington was the first U.S. president. He helped form the United States. Jefferson was the third president. He helped the country grow. Lincoln was the sixteenth president. He kept the country together during the American Civil War (1861–1865). Roosevelt was the twenty-sixth president. He helped protect the people and land of the United States.

◄ *The faces of Presidents George Washington, Thomas Jefferson, Theodore Roosevelt, and Abraham Lincoln are carved into the mountain.*

How Was Such a Large Sculpture Carved?

Borglum began the work in 1927. First he made a **model** of the sculpture. Then, to find out how big each part would need to be on the mountain, he measured the model.

About 400 workers helped Borglum carve the sculpture. They worked from April until late fall every year for fourteen years.

They used **dynamite** to blast off large pieces of rock. They added the details with **drills** and **chisels**. They worked until the rock had a smooth white surface.

◄ *Borglum made a model of the sculpture in his studio.*

What Problems Did Borglum Face?

Safety was important to Borglum. The men had to hang from **cables** off the side of the mountain to do their work. They hung hundreds of feet above the ground.

Using dynamite was dangerous too. Borglum always made sure all workers were off the mountain before setting off the blast.

Borglum also had to be careful not to make many mistakes with the dynamite. There was no way to put the rock back if he blasted off too much of it.

◀ *Stone carvers faced great dangers working on Mount Rushmore.*

Were Changes Made to the Sculpture?

Borglum could not always carve the sculpture exactly as he had planned. In some places, the rock was not strong enough. The granite had cracks or holes. Sometimes he needed to move a nose or an eye to be sure it was carved into solid rock.

Borglum had planned to show each president down to the waist. But parts of the rock were not as strong as he had hoped. So he decided that the heads were enough.

◀ *Borglum sometimes worked with the stone carvers to make changes to the sculpture.*

How Big Is Mount Rushmore?

Mount Rushmore is a mountain that is 5,725 feet (1,746 meters) high. That is more than a mile! George Washington's head is as high as a five-story building, or two school buses.

Walk about twenty steps. That distance is about the width of each mouth and the length of each nose on the monument. Each eye is as long as a car.

◄ *The heads are as tall as a five-story building.*

How Can You See Mount Rushmore?

You can visit Mount Rushmore National Memorial. It is in western South Dakota. First you walk up the Avenue of Flags. It is lined with the flags of fifty states and six territories. Then you can view the monument from the Grandview Terrace.

At the Lincoln Borglum Museum, you can learn how the monument was made. You can see the tools and models at the Sculptor's **Studio**. You can take a long walk up the Presidential Trail to get a closer view of the faces. After dark, you can see the monument lit up.

◀ *The Avenue of Flags lines the sidewalk leading to the Visitor Center.*

What Does Mount Rushmore Mean to People?

Mount Rushmore meant a great deal to Borglum. When he died in 1941, his son, Lincoln Borglum, helped finish the faces on the monument.

The Mount Rushmore National Memorial means a lot to the people who see it too. The faces on the mountain make people remember the great men who helped create America. The sculpture reminds Americans of why they love their country.

◄ *Millions of people travel to South Dakota each year to see Mount Rushmore.*

Glossary

cables—strong ropes

chisels—tools used to cut small pieces of rock

drills—tools used to make deep holes

dynamite—an explosive used to blast away pieces of rock

model—a small copy of something

monument—a sculpture or building created to honor someone or something

studio—an artist's workplace

Did You Know?

• At first, people didn't recognize Thomas Jefferson's face. They thought it was George Washington's wife Martha!

• The huge pile of broken rock that Borglum blasted off the mountain still lies at the base of the monument.

• Washington's head was finished first. Jefferson was next, then Lincoln, and finally Roosevelt.

Want to Know More?

At the Library

Gabriel, Luke S. *Mount Rushmore: From Mountain to Monument*. Chanhassen, Minn.: The Child's World, 2000.

Giblin, James Cross. *Thomas Jefferson: A Picture Book Biography*. New York: Scholastic, 1994.

Lepthien, Emilie U. *South Dakota*. Danbury, Conn.: Children's Press. 1996.

Turner, Ann Warren. *Abe Lincoln Remembers*. New York: HarperCollins Children's Books, 2001.

Usel, T.M. *George Washington*. Mankato, Minn.: Bridgestone Books, 1999.

On the Web

National Park Service Mount Rushmore National Memorial
http://www.nps.gov/moru/
For information about the memorial and what to see when you visit

Travel South Dakota: Mount Rushmore
http://www.travelsd.com/parks/rushmore/
For a complete history of the monument, a photo album, and information about how to visit

Through the Mail

Mount Rushmore National Memorial
P.O. Box 268
Keystone, SD 57751
For information about the national memorial and how to visit

On the Road

Mount Rushmore National Memorial
P.O. Box 268
Keystone, SD 57751
605/574-3171

Index

About the Author

Dana Meachen Rau is the author of more than fifty books for children, including historical fiction, storybooks, nonfiction, biographies, and early readers. Dana also works as a children's book editor and illustrator and lives with her husband, Chris, and son, Charlie, in Farmington, Connecticut.